One Key Can Open Many Doors

The answer to all those problems may be right in front of you!

DR. HOWARD MURAD, M.D.

Wisdom Waters Press
1000 Wilshire Blvd., #1500
Los Angeles, CA 90017-2457

Quantity sales. Special discounts are available on quantity purchases by corporations, associations, and others. For details, contact the "Special Sales Department" at the address above.

Printed in China

ISBN-10: 1-939642-24-8
ISBN-13: 978-1-939642-24-0

First Edition

Murad

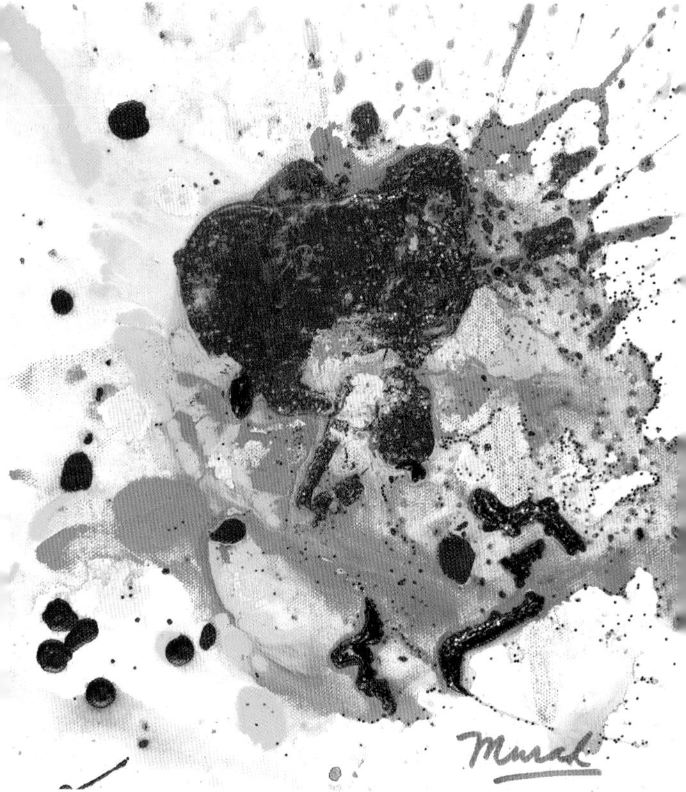

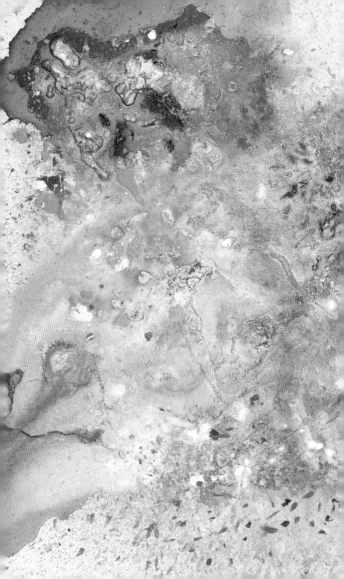

When it seems like life is an endless array of problems, don't despair. Your troubles likely stem from a single root cause. Fix that and you may just fix them all.

ABOUT
THE ART

Self-expression is essential to human health and happiness. The author was reminded of that several years ago when he discovered a new outlet for his own irrepressible creative drive: painting. Interestingly enough, he's never taken any formal art classes, but his canvases are nonetheless sophisticated. His modernist style makes pure chance a key element in the artistic process. This results in explosions of color and form that expand the limits of imagination. Dr. Murad created the illustrations in this book hoping they would help you expand your imagination and envision a better tomorrow.

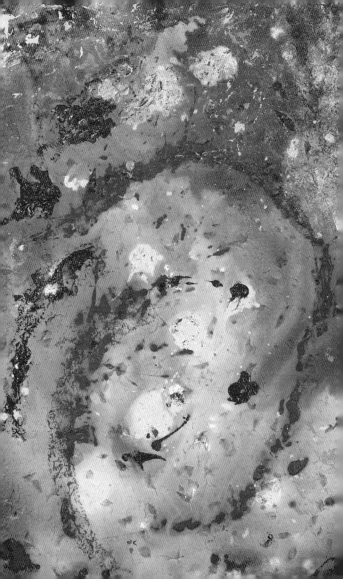

Murad

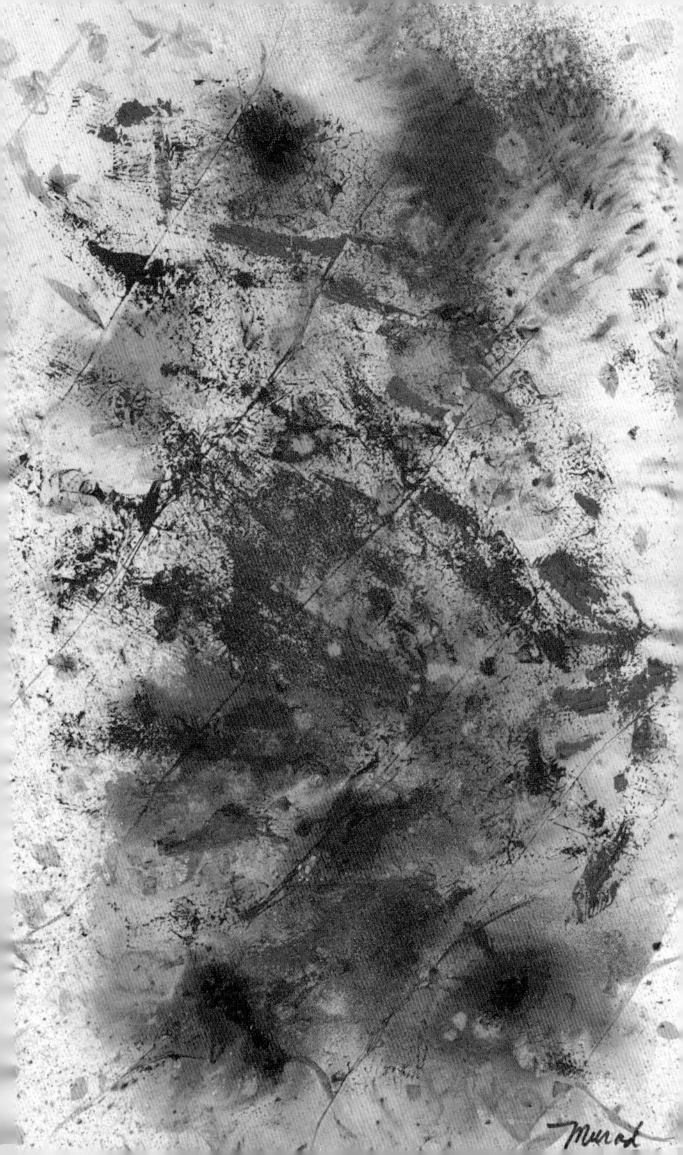

ONE KEY CAN OPEN MANY DOORS

Sometimes a person's life has taken an unfortunate turn and they just haven't realized yet that it's time to start down a new road. That was certainly the case with Elisa, a young lady who came to my dermatology office is Los Angeles a few years ago with a fairly typical skin condition. I've successfully treated many, many patients with complaints similar to hers, but in Elisa's case, there seemed to be a lot more going on.

As we talked, it became evident that she was not a particularly healthy or happy person. She wasn't sleeping well and had little enthusiasm for either her work or personal life. Elisa revealed that these and a host of other symptoms, both physical and emotional, had emerged more than a year earlier about the time she had gone through a separation and divorce—no doubt, a very painful experience. I suggested that the divorce might be indirectly related to some of her current problems.

"That may be so," she said. "But there is nothing I can do now to change the past."

True enough, but as Elisa would soon discover, there was plenty she could do to change the way she *related* to the past. I treated her for her skin condition and she left. At the time, I had no idea of how she would respond to our conversation or what action, if any, she would take on what we had discussed.

I did not see her again until several weeks later when she came to my office for a follow-up visit. Her skin condition had completely cleared and she seemed almost a different person. Her voice, which had been flat and lifeless before, was now full of vitality. She said she was sleeping soundly. Her emotional state and her health had taken a dramatic turn in the right direction.

"I feel great!" she said.

How had this happened? She told me the story. As it turned out, the suggestion that her divorce might somehow be related to her current symptoms had unlocked something in her heart. By the time she had arrived home from her first appointment, Elisa had decided that she had to let go of some feelings she had clung to for far too long.

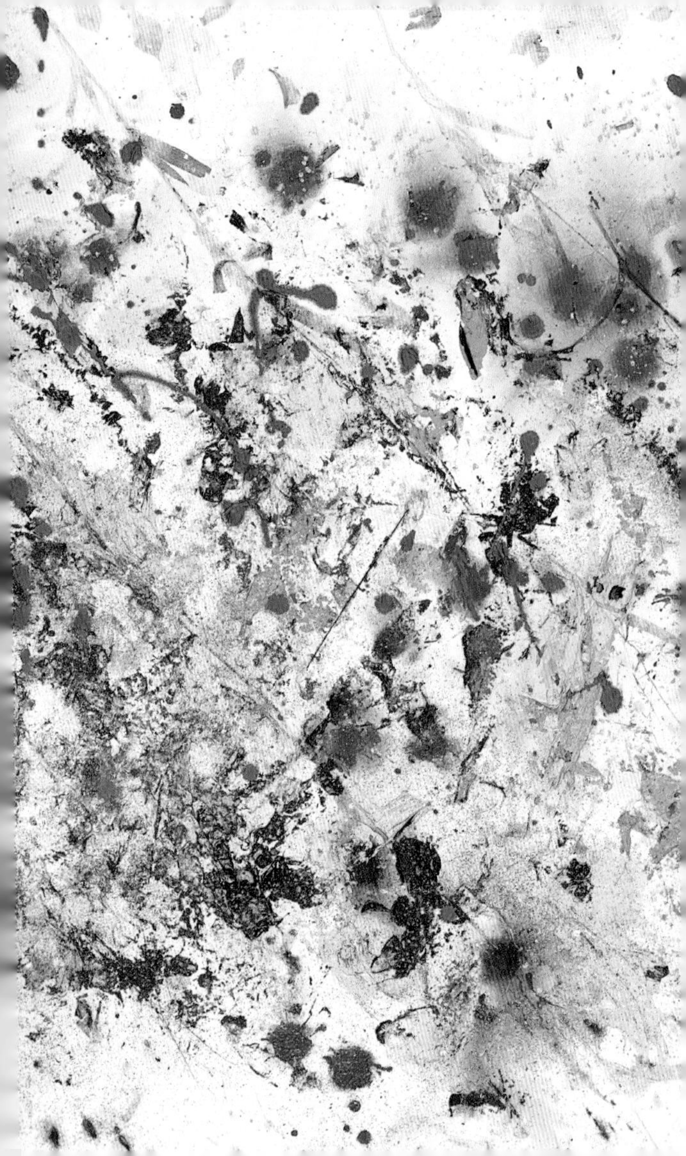

She threw open the door of a closet that was positively bulging with mementos of her married life: gifts, photographs, holiday decorations, even some dried flowers from a special celebration. She packed it all up—every package, picture, and petal—and threw it out or gave it away. She told me she had never felt a sense of relief and release like she did after she cleaned out that closet.

Before long she had cleaned out all the other closets and drawers in the house. Then she moved out of the house altogether and away from the neighborhood she had lived in with her former husband. She got a different job, bought new clothes and, in time, found a new and more rewarding love relationship. I believe she is now living very happily in a town just north of Los Angeles, and the key to all of this was cleaning out a closet.

Root Causes

Over the decades since I began practicing medicine, I've treated over 50,000 patients, and I've done the very best I could for them. I've always tried to make them look better, feel better, and live healthier, happier lives. One of the ways I've done this is to focus on root causes.

Medical science has shown that many seemingly unrelated symptoms can be traced to a single disease. When patients come to us with a whole range of complaints—say, as many as ten—we try to focus in on the most important problem. Instead of giving them ten separate diagnoses, we try to give them one. We ask ourselves which of these concerns is closest to the source of their various troubles. This is not always the right approach, but more often than not it produces the desired result. We treat the root cause and the patient gets better. Most or all of the symptoms begin to clear up and go away.

Often a standard medical prescription won't fix anything. It may help with one or more of the patient's symptoms, while the others may remain stubbornly resistant to treatment. This may be because the real problem lies within the patient's daily life or their whole approach to living. Perhaps they have a bad diet—so many of us do. Maybe they don't get enough exercise—lots of people don't get any at all. Or maybe they are under far too much stress.

Our lives today are awash in what I call *cultural stress:* troubling news on television, countless emails to answer, work pressures, deadlines to meet, meetings to attend, or just the day-to-day demands of maintaining a home and keeping up with acquaintances. It can all be far too much, and *it can make people sick*.

Rather than helping to bring people together, smartphones and the Internet tend to isolate us. We are naturally social beings, but we spend more and more time alone, replying to text messages, pouring over emails, or playing video games. The isolation this causes is another very potent form of cultural stress.

Keys to a Better Life

The key to living a healthier, happier life could be as simple as a better diet. We all need to eat more fresh fruits and vegetables. These are rich in the structural water our body and brain require.

The key to opening up a better life could be pulling on a pair of hiking shoes and going for a walk in the country. Exercise

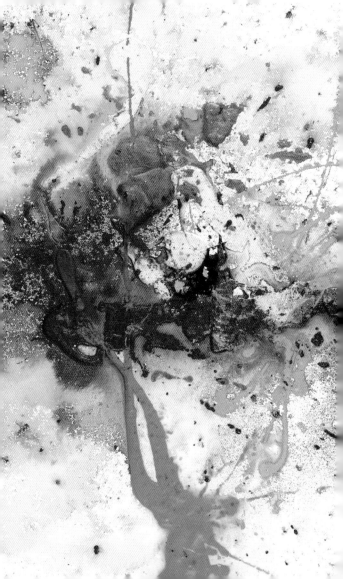

can do our physical and emotional health a world of good. So can fresh air, open skies, and scenic vistas.

The key may be found in seeking the companionship of other people. If you don't seek it, you won't find it. You may need to set aside time when you step away from your phone, television, and other devices.

The key may lie in doing whatever we can to avoid the tsunami of cultural stress that threatens to overwhelm us all. Take a deep breath and don't load up every moment of every single day with must-do activities. There's always time to get things done, and if there's not, that's okay, too.

Or as was the case with Elisa, the key may be hidden in the dark recesses of an over-stuffed closet. The important thing is to look. Whatever the key may be, if we look hard enough, it can be found.

Perhaps the key for you may be opening up your natural creativity. Art therapy works. That's why more and more hospitals and clinics are using it to improve both the emotional and physical health of their patients. Art encourages people to see outside themselves and take a fresh perspective on life. It allows light to enter. To experience that light, make time for art, music, poetry, or whatever creative activity brings you joy.

Is there something holding you back? Give it some thought, and if you come to the conclusion the answer is yes, make some changes. You just may find that you've opened the door, not on a closet, but to a much healthier and happier life!

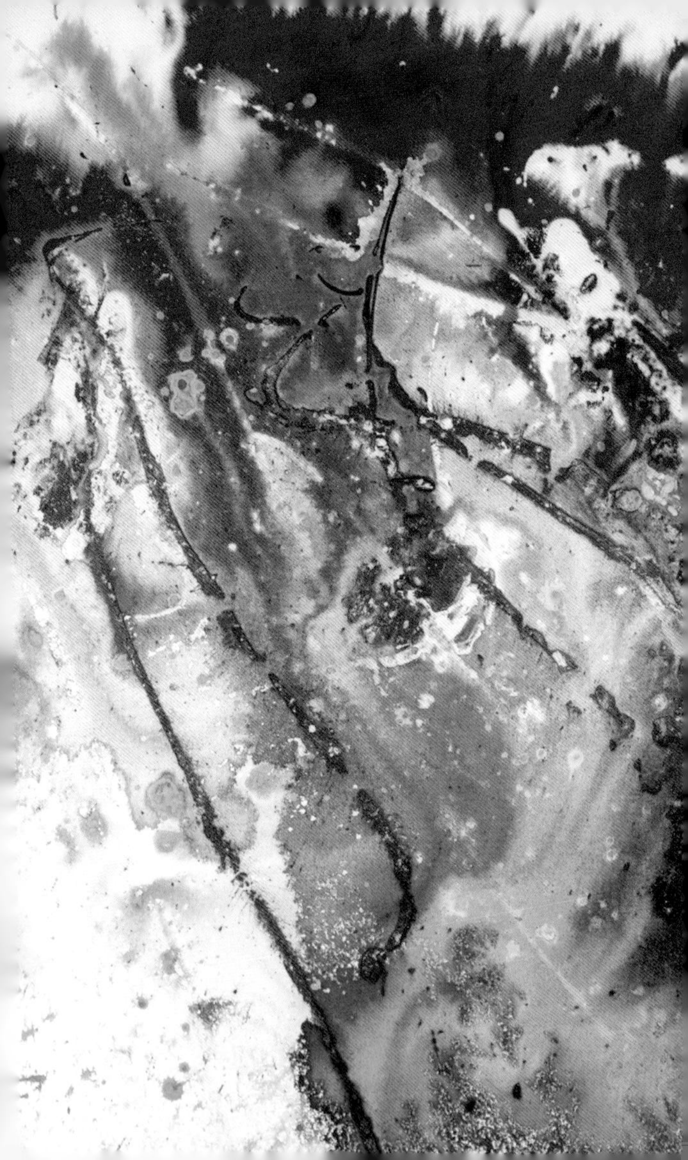

LIFE IS ART

When I create paintings like the ones you see in this book, I make a few marks on a canvas, add some colors, and spray them with water. The water is allowed to interact with the art in a more or less random way, and this often carries the artwork in a totally unexpected direction. How's it going to turn out? I don't know.

My life has been like that too. I started out thinking I wanted to be an engineer. When that didn't work out for me, I went into pharmacy and that, in turn, led me into medicine. Whatever happened along the way, I always felt life was carrying me somewhere. Life is a canvas, you see. You make your mark on it and then flow with it. If you allow it to flow in a way that makes sense, your life will be a work of art.

Interestingly, I didn't start painting until 2008 when retinal surgery forced me to spend a rather challenging month always looking down. My wife, Loralee, suggested I try my hand at art to help me pass the time. I followed her advice and found that expressing myself with color on canvas was far more invigorating than I had ever imagined. I truly believe that painting helped me heal faster, and after that experience, I began to incorporate art into my overall skin care and general health philosophies. Along with an emphasis on personal creativity, my approach includes a diet rich in water and whole foods, appropriate skin care products, targeted supplements, rest, and plenty of exercise.

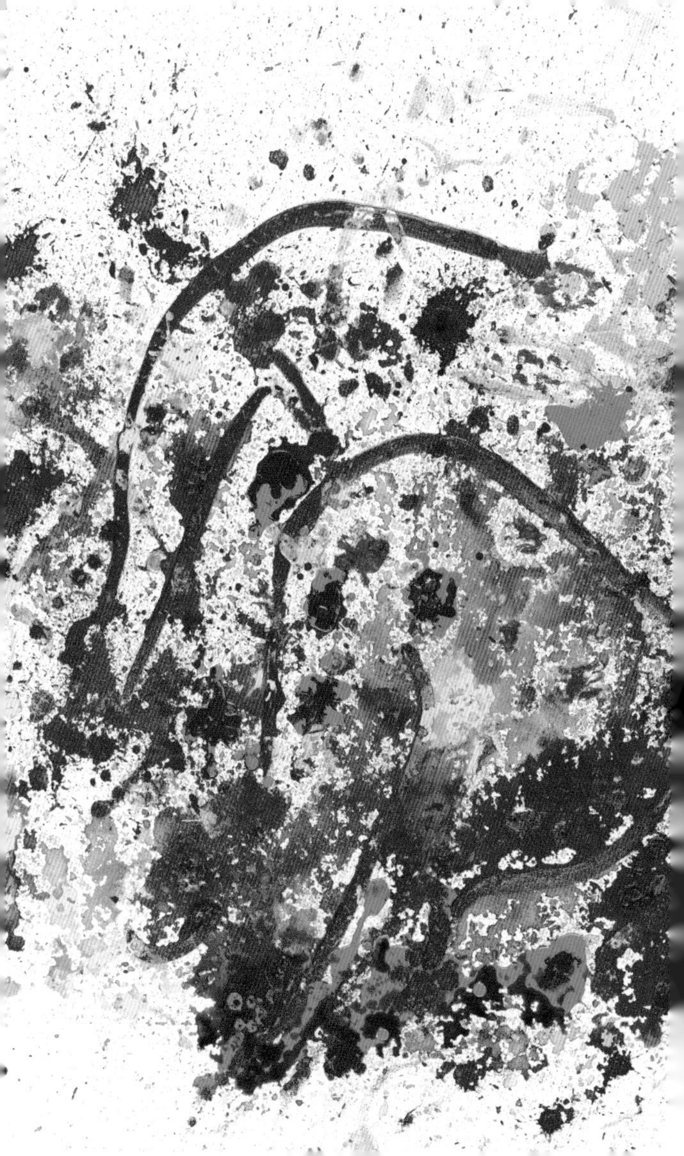

It also includes a positive attitude. If you smile a lot and turn a happy face toward other people, you're going to look a lot more attractive. There is an emotional component to both your appearance and your health, and when you are creative your emotions are allowed to run free. If you have an engaging outlet for your natural creativity, you will sleep better, be more vibrant, and smile a lot more.

When I consult with patients, we don't just talk about individual skin conditions. These are always linked to other problems and concerns, so we discuss a whole range of health-related issues. We also discuss various ways people can express themselves creatively. This will improve their overall wellbeing, and I try to send them home with a plan that takes personal creativity into consideration.

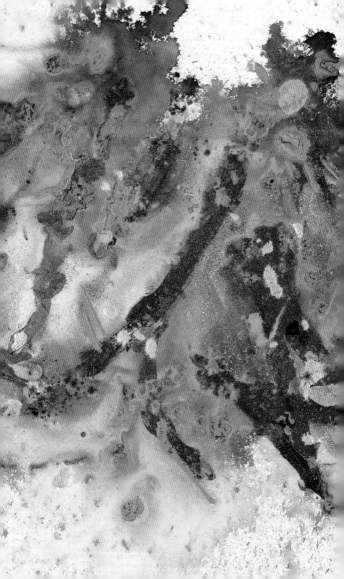

SIMPLE WORDS OF WISDOM

Occasionally, I have what I believe to be a meaningful insight into the human quest for health and happiness. Usually these insights occur to me when I'm working with patients or talking with a friend. Over the years I've collected hundreds of these insights, and I now think of them simply as my "sayings."

When patients visit my office to take part in our Inclusive Health program, I share several of the sayings with them. They may focus on one or another of the insights, and sometimes they say, "You know, I haven't

27

thought of that before." It's almost impossible so say which of the insights will interest them, and maybe that isn't important since most of the sayings are related in one way or another. The sayings all have in common the idea that you *can* change your life for the better. It's all a matter of how you approach the challenges of living. Here are a few insights that I hope will encourage you to unlock the door to a better life.

Listen to yourself so you can pay attention to your needs

Our bodies have a lot to teach us. But if we're not listening, we'll never learn. We may be placing ourselves under far too much stress. We may be working much too hard. We may be eating too much of all the wrong foods. Our bodies invariably respond to these things, and yours may be crying out for change. If so, you should be paying attention.

Sometimes more ends up being less

Acquisitiveness, the endless drive to acquire more and more material possessions, can be a trap. Very soon, it may reach the point when nothing is enough. We should strive to own only those things that make us happy or allow us to make others happy.

Turn the rest of your life into the best of your life

Your best years are still ahead of you. Even if that turns out not to be true, it sure helps to believe it. And I do believe it. There are always fresh adventures and wondrous new discoveries out there on the horizon. Embrace them, and you can be sure that the best is yet to come.

Isolation can be a self-imposed prison

The population of the earth grows each and every day and big cities get even bigger, but ironically, people are more isolated

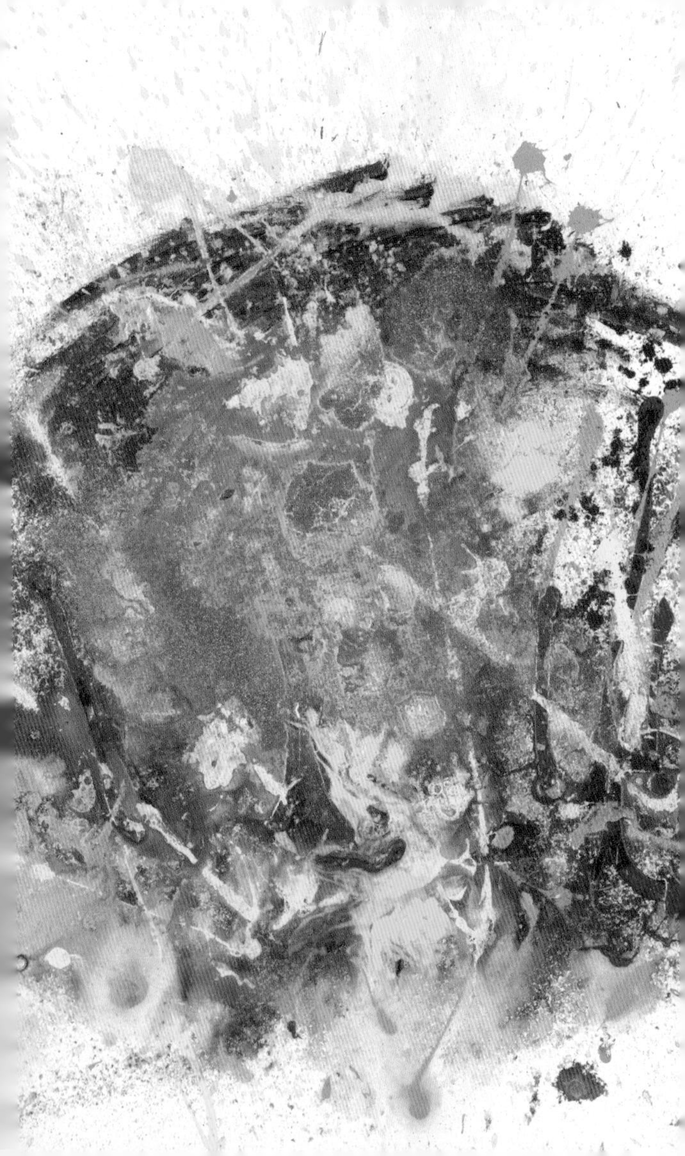

than ever before. The demands of modern life separate us from our families, from our friends, from everybody, and we live an increasingly solitary existence. Computers have made it possible for us to communicate with machines and other computers all around the world but not necessarily with other people. It's not unusual for us to spend the whole day at a computer and hardly speak to another person. We send each other text messages even if we happen to work in the same building, maybe even in adjacent offices. Instead of real flesh-and-blood friends, we have a computer-driven social network. Along with this techno-isolation has come a very deep and personal loneliness, a sense that something vital is missing from our lives. Don't allow yourself to be pulled down into a well of isolation. Climb up into the open air and reach out to other people. They will welcome you.

Don't substitute overeating for proper cultural stress management

Overeating is not just a *bad* habit. It can be a highly destructive, even deadly one. Often, overeating is a response to cultural stress, the emotional and physical pressure placed on us by the demands and dissonance of 21st-century life. We exist under a constant barrage of cellphone calls, emails, and distressing news on cable television and the radio. Maybe our overeating is telling us to get out of the stop-and-go techno-traffic, pull off the road, and breathe a little. Then, we can take the time to taste our food and enjoy it rather than gobble it down.

Returning to your youth is the path to happiness

Have you ever noticed that young people often tend to be happy regardless of their circumstances? That's because they *are* young. They don't doubt their capabilities,

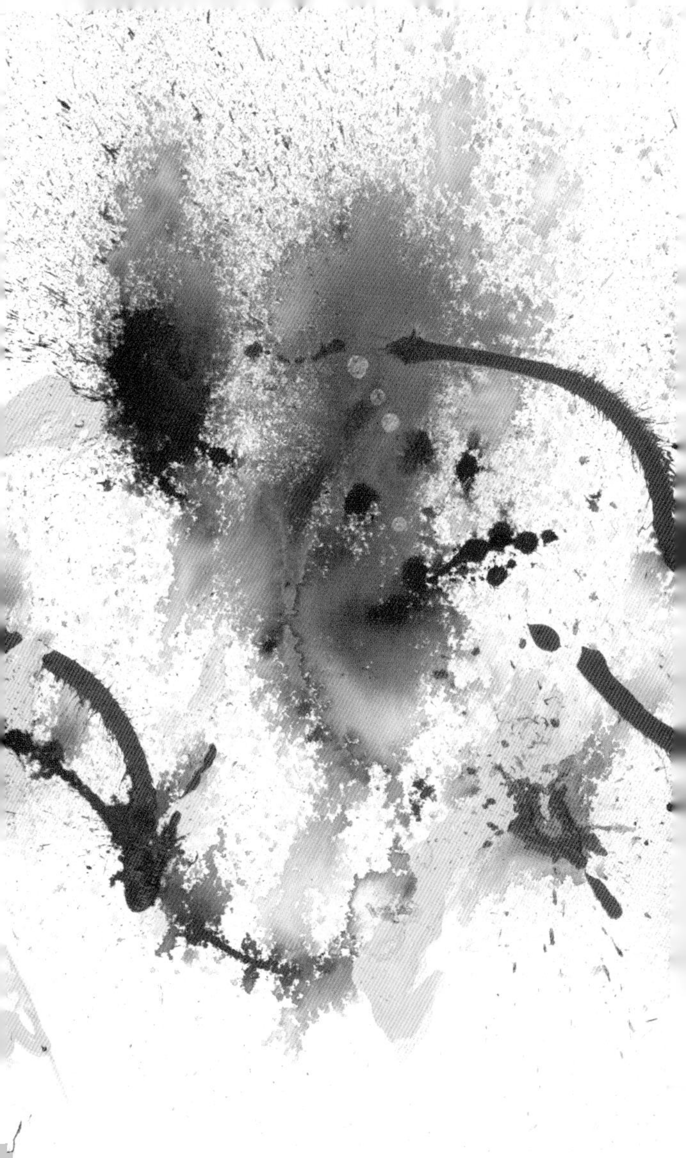

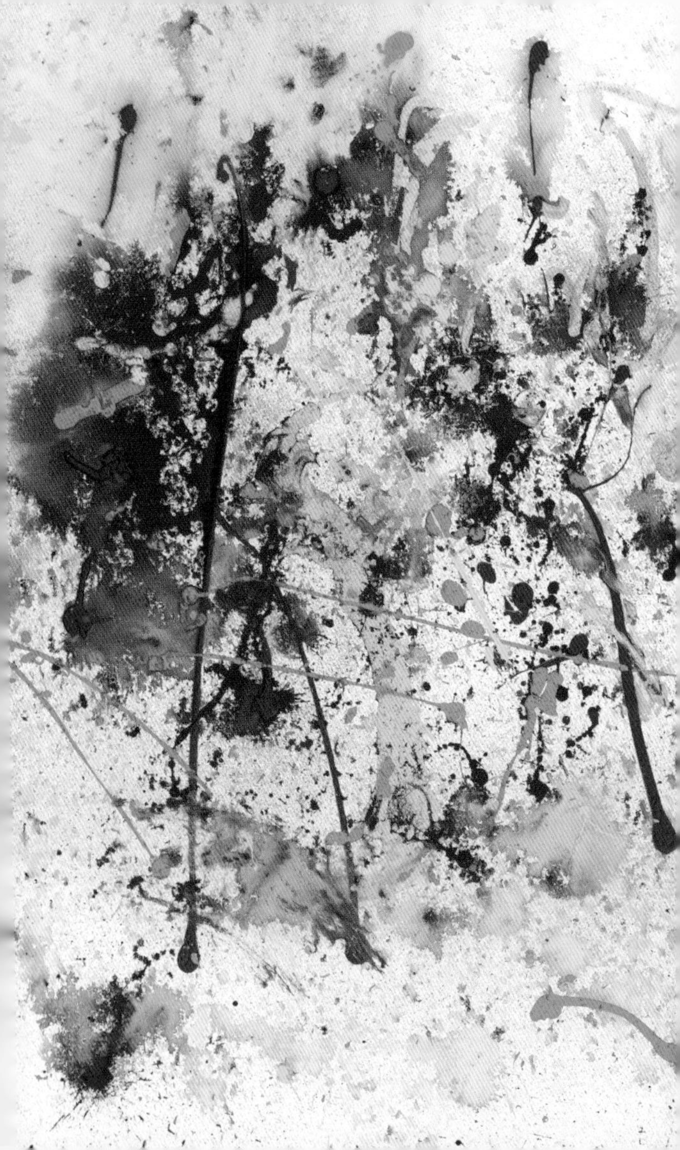

they don't set limits on themselves, and they're enthusiastic about almost everything. You can be like that, too, no matter what your age. It is possible to return to your youth spiritually, emotionally and, to a large extent, physically as well.

Don't focus on the minutia in life

You've heard the adage that "he can't see the forest for the trees." If you get too caught up in the details of life, you'll lose sight of the bigger, more important things. Keep in mind that success in almost any endeavor requires you to see the big picture and grasp the full sweep of events.

Give yourself an opportunity to have a transformation

Most of the key positive changes in our lives come about as the result of personal transformations. These transformations don't just happen by themselves. We have to be open to them and to all the possibilities they represent.

Water-rich foods—the best diet plan

If you want to look good, feel good, and lose weight, consider switching to a diet high in raw fruits, vegetables, and other water-rich foods. Scientific research, including my own work with thousands of individual patients, has shown a direct link between good health and high levels of cellular water. Basically, the more you increase your cellular water, the healthier you will become. The opposite is also true. When you lose cellular water, you open the door to aging and disease.

Happiness is the best facelift

Happiness can make you and your skin glow in a way that no cosmetic or surgical treatment can match. If you feel content with yourself and your surroundings, you are likely to look good, too.

Restore youth

If you maintain a youthful attitude throughout your life, you can look good, feel good, and experience success regardless of your chronological age. If you've lost that youthful feeling, don't despair. It can be restored. All that's required is to go back to doing things the way you did them when you were young, with the same free spirit. Remember, youth springs from within.

Make every day a vacation
by choosing a life you love

When you are on holiday, you begin to look at things that you never saw before and you start doing things for the sheer joy of doing them. Life should be like that all the time. A vacation is thought of as an opportunity for relaxation, regeneration, and reflection. But you need those things constantly, not just once or twice a year. The best way to turn your day-to-day life into a constant vacation is to choose a life partner and a job that are right for you.

Champion your own decisions

Making decisions is hard. There's always the risk of making a bad decision. Some people get permanently stuck because they avoid making any decisions at all. You'll never succeed in life that way. Decision making takes courage, but how can you make the right one unless you're brave enough to take the risk of getting it wrong? Once you've made a key decision, stand behind it and make sure others know where you stand and why. If you don't champion your own decisions, who will?

Turn transitions into opportunities for positive change

Important positive changes in our lives often come about as the result of personal transformations. In most cases, however,

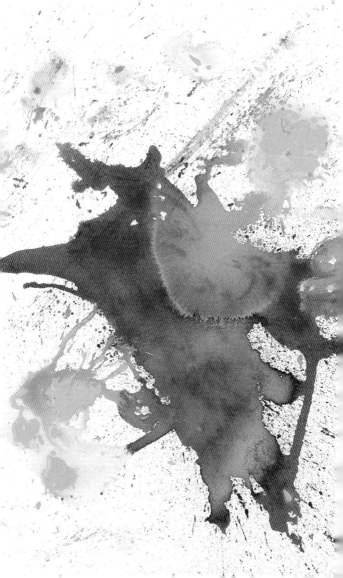

these transformations will not produce positive results unless we are prepared to take advantage of the opportunities they present. We must be open to change and willing to embrace the new possibilities it offers.

Create new opportunities
without fear of failure

Sometimes opportunity just happens. But more often than not, you have to create your own opportunity. Perhaps this can be done by changing jobs or locations or by generating a fresh idea and making it a reality. Be ready to try new things without being afraid of what others may think. Likely they'll respect your willingness to take a risk, and if you are successful, they'll celebrate it with you. Keep in mind that failure will not diminish you in any way and that you can always try again.

Don't just think out of the box, but rather think as if there were no box

All too often our focus is too narrow even when we are trying to be inventive. Rather than create something entirely new, we allow ourselves to be boxed in by old ways of thinking. We concentrate on limited goals such as buying a new car or getting a promotion when what we really should be seeking is a complete change in our approach to life. Instead of pursuing a promotion, perhaps you should consider going into a whole new profession or creating a unique endeavor all your own.

Real success is when you do what you are told you can't do

When other people say you won't succeed, don't listen to them. Don't listen to your internal critic either. Instead, give yourself positive messages—you *are* good enough, you *will* succeed, and you *will*

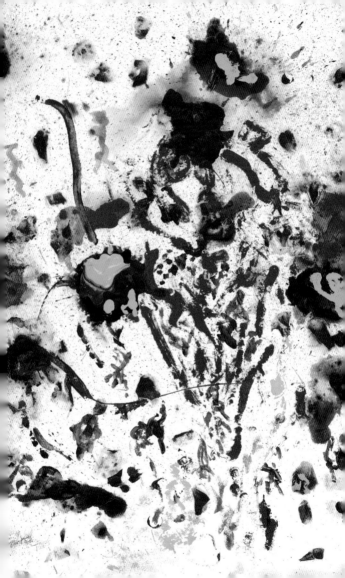

accomplish your goals. To realize your true potential, free yourself from negativity. Professional athletes and other successful people always try to emphasize the positive. Follow their example and you'll have more self-confidence and greater success in everything you attempt. Then, when you accomplish what others have been saying was impossible, that's real success!

Give yourself permission to be happy
Some people experience very little happiness in their lives because they don't believe they are supposed to be happy. They're waiting for someone to give them permission to be happy. Happiness does not require a permit, and you don't need anyone's permission. You can and should give it to yourself.

DR. HOWARD MURAD'S INCLUSIVE HEALTH APPROACH

A prominent Los Angeles physician, Dr. Howard Murad has successfully treated over 50,000 patients. Drawing on his training as both a pharmacist and physician, he has developed a popular and highly effective line of skin care products that has won praise from health- and beauty-conscious people everywhere. A practitioner not just of medicine but of the philosophy of health, he has written dozens of books and articles, earning him a worldwide reputation as an authority on slowing the aging process.

Dr. Murad's unique approach to medicine involves a concept he calls Inclusive Health. An alternative to traditional medical practice with its emphasis on the "spot treatment" of individual conditions or illnesses, the Inclusive Health approach treats the whole patient. Among other things, it takes into consideration the patient's diet, lifestyle, and emotional state as well as intercellular water—the hydration level of cells.

Years of painstaking research and experience with thousands of patients have shown Dr. Murad that human health and happiness are directly linked to the ability of cells to retain water. A poor diet and the stress of day-to-day living can damage the all-important membranes that form cell walls. Over time, the membranes become broken and porous, causing the cells to leak water and lose vitality. This in turn

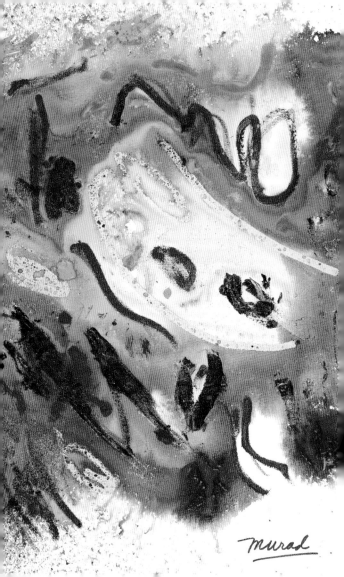

murad

leads to accelerated aging and a wide variety of diseases and syndromes.

In his groundbreaking bestseller *The Water Secret*, published in 2010, Dr. Murad outlined how to stop this process—and reverse it—through Inclusive Healthcare. This approach has three essential components. The first involves good skin care practices, the second, a healthy diet emphasizing raw fruits and vegetables, and the third an overall reduction in stress combined with a more youthful and creative outlook on life.

The third component, which emphasizes our emotional state, may be the most challenging part of the Inclusive Health treatment process for people to adopt. The breakneck pace of modern life with its freeways, computers, cell phones, and fast-paced living places upon us an enormous amount of what Dr. Murad describes as *cultural stress.*

To deal with this runaway stress we live increasingly structured lives that are less and less open to the free play and creativity that make life worth living. We can choose not to live this way. But reducing stress and embracing a more youthful outlook often involves major shifts in lifestyle—changes in jobs, accommodations, locales, hobbies, habits, and relationships. It may even require a complete personal transformation of the sort sometimes identified with a single galvanizing moment of self-awareness. You may experience a transforming moment like that while walking on a beach, creating a work of art, driving through the countryside, or maybe just stretching your arms after a long night's sleep. Who can say?

To help his patients awaken to a better life, Dr. Murad has composed a substantial collection of personal insights or sayings that deliver bits of health advice, philosophy, and wisdom straight up, like strong coffee. In his medical practice, Dr. Murad shares these brief meditations with patients as a way of encouraging them to improve their health by adopting more youthful, creative, and health-conscious lifestyles. You may find them similarly inspirational. In addition to the insights you have already encountered in this book, here are a few others that you may find interesting and useful.

Make an appointment with yourself.

———————————————

Reconcile yourself to the truth and then make the best of it.

The fastest way to improve your mood is to smile.

Developing your passion is a major step in the journey to happiness.

Be happy when you see happiness in others.

If you put what you are worrying about in perspective, it's probably no big deal.

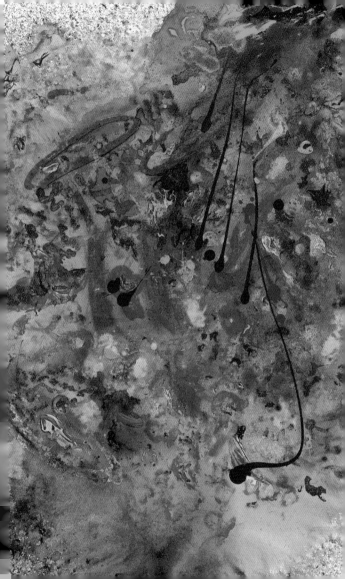

Allow the accidents in life to have a powerful impact on you.

Unlock your hidden potential.

Encourage your free spirit.

The path to isolation begins with the Internet.

Spontaneity leads to a more fulfilling life.

Art is medicine.

———————————

Healing is central to health.

———————————

If you can think it, it could happen.

———————————

*The right answer is not always
the right answer.*

———————————

*Positive self-talk encourages a
positive outcome.*

———————————

*Allow your disability to
transform your abilities.*

Before you get angry,
consider the cost.

Forgive yourself first
before you forgive others,
and then both of you can heal.

When you love others,
you will become loved.

Embrace the little things you do;
they may become really big things.

Dear reader,
Please share this book with others or give it as a gift to family, friends, or business associates. Also be sure to look for Dr. Murad's other inspirational "little" books:

Be Imperfect, Live Longer

Give Yourself Permission to Be Happy

Honor Yourself

The Best Is Yet to Come

Why Have a Bad Day
When You Can Have a Good Day?